# TILLICH'S RESPONSE TO FREUD:
# A CHRISTIAN ANSWER TO THE
# FREUDIAN CRITIQUE OF RELIGION

## JOHN M. PERRY

**UNIVERSITY
PRESS OF
AMERICA**

Lanham • New York • London

To my parents –
with affection and gratitude.

# ACKNOWLEDGMENTS

The author wishes to thank the following: W.W. Norton & Co., Inc., for permission to quote copyrighted material from *The Future of an Illusion*, by Sigmund Freud, translated from the German and edited by James Strachey, copyright ©1961 by James Strachey; The University of Chicago Press for permission to quote copyrighted material from *Systematic Theology*, 3 vols., by Paul Tillich: Volume I ©1951 by The University of Chicago, Volume II ©1957 by The University of Chicago, Volume III ©1963 by the University of Chicago.

# CONTENTS

# INTRODUCTION

AMONG MODERN THINKERS WHO HAVE GRAP-
pled with the idea of God, one of the most disturbing was
Sigmund Freud. Freud was a creative innovator of the first
rank whose seminal insights into the human psyche are still
widely influential. However, as is well known, Freud sometimes wandered from the path of his true expertise,
psychology, and made philosophical pronouncements of an
atheistic kind. As a consequence, his ideas about the
psychological factors involved in religious experience are
suspect in the eyes of some Christians and are rejected in
their entirety.

Paul Tillich is considered by many to be the modern
Christan theolgian who best understood Freudian psychoanalysis.[1] Tillich pointed out that it would be wrong to
refuse to listen to what Freud said about *psychological
reality,* simply because we know in advance that we will not
agree with some of his philosophical conclusions about *ultimate reality.* As a Christian theologian whose experience
was significantly different than Freud's, Tillich predictably
rejected Freud's atheism. He was convinced, nevertheless,
that Freud's challenging views contained much that was of

great value to Christian theology.

In his "Autobiographical Reflections," Tillich tells us that he became acquainted with psychoanalysis as a young man in his native Germany and followed its development with interest.[2] After he emigrated to the United States in 1933 and began teaching at Union Theological Seminary in New York, his earlier interest deepened. As a result of seminars dealing with psychoanalysis and personal friendships with a number of analysts, he became keenly interested in the relation between depth psychology and theology and concluded: "I do not think that it is possible today to elaborate a Christian doctrine of the Christian man, without using the immense material brought forth by depth psychology."[3]

The modest work which follows presents the salient aspects of Tillich's response to Freud in the hope that this will help the nonspecialist to see more clearly which of Freud's ideas make a positive contribution to Christian faith understanding and which do not. Since Freud preceded Tillich historically, the first chapter will summarize Freud's ideas about God and religion. The four following chapters will deal with Tillich's rejoinder.

The reader should be advised that the whole of Tillich's complex thought about God will not be reviewed in this small volume; only those of his ideas which lend themselves to dialogue with the Freudian critique of religion will be considered. Those who wish to know more about Tillich's doctrine of God will find a full exposition in volume I of his *Systematic Theology*.

Since the chapters that follow are an attempt to bring the views of Freud and Tillich into dialogue, and since both men antedated the feminist movement, no attempt has been made to reconcile the paraphrasing of their thought with contemporary concerns about sexist language; to do so would distort their characteristic modes of thought and deny history.                                        ODaU-M

## *NOTES*

1. Peter Homans, "Toward a Psychology of Religion: By Way of Freud and Tillich," in *the Dialogue Between Theology and Psychology,* ed. by Peter Homans (Chicago: The University of Chicago Press, 1968), 64; Earl A. Loomis, Jr., "The Psychiatric Legacy of Paul Tillich," in *The Intellectual Legacy of Paul Tillich,* ed. by James R. Lyons (Detroit: Wayne State University Press, 1969), 81-96.

2. Paul Tillich, "Autobiographical Reflections," in *The Theology of Paul Tillich,* ed. by Charles W. Kegley and Robert W. Bretall (New York: The Macmillan Company, 1964), 18-19.

3. *Ibid.,* 19.

# CHAPTER ONE

# Freud's View of God as Projection and Religious Faith as Illusion

## I.

IN THE COURSE OF HIS PSYCHOANALYTICAL IN-
vestigations, Freud noticed that the neurotics he worked
with consistently manifested an infantile dependence on
parental authority figures and their attitudes.[1] This led Freud
to explore carefully the relationship between parents and
children and resulted in his formulating the following
theory:

> ...children regularly direct their sexual wishes towards
> their nearest relatives – in the first place, therefore,
> towards their father and mother, and afterwards
> towards their brothers and sisters. The first object of a
> boy's love is his mother, and of a girl's her father. . . .
> The other parent is felt as a disturbing rival and not in-
> frequently viewed with strong hostility.[2]

Freud called the triangular relationship which results in
a small child becoming strongly attracted to the parent of
the opposite sex and hostile toward the parent of the same
sex the Oedipus complex.[3] He attached extraordinary sig-
nificance to its influence: "...I should like to insist that...the
beginnings of religion, morals, society and art converge in

1

the Oedipus complex."[4] The Oedipal conflict of early childhood was considered by Freud to be the primordial source of the experiences, unconscious memories, and attitudes from which mankind has derived its idea of God and the beliefs and practices of religion.

The Oedipus complex and its ramifications were usually discussed by Freud from the male point of view. He observed that the first love object of every little boy is inevitably his mother, since she is the primary source of his need satisfaction and security. But the small and helpless child soon becomes aware that he has a powerful rival for his mother's time and affection in the person of his father, with whom he cannot hope to compete;[5] to the child the father seems a godlike giant, omnipotent and omniscient, whose wrath and punitive power are terrible indeed.[6]

The child's experience of his own weakness and his father's seeming omnipotence is heightened not only by their disproportionate sizes but also by the fact that intense affect in early childhood is experienced as virtually absolute.[7] The small child is still lacking the learning experiences necessary for qualifying such affect and reducing it to the measure that is realistically proportionate to a given situation. (For this reason the father image preserved in earliest unconscious memory is endowed with unlimited power.) Fear of the father's displeasure and need for his protection gradually induce the child to repress his hostility and submit to the father's prior claim to the time and affection of the mother.[8]

In connection with his theory of Oedipal conflict between father and son, Freud advanced the controversial view that soon after man's emergence from the evolutionary process primal sons who had reached physical maturity banded together and killed the primal father in order to have access to the females fiercely guarded as his personal preserve. But the victory of the primal sons over their murdered father turned out to be hollow, for the powerful father lived on ineradicably in memory as both feared and desired. His lingering presence (in the superego) was still feared as the dread punisher of incest and desired as the powerful protector from threatening danger. The intense guilt and anxiety that resulted from the acting out of their Oedipal desires eventually induced the sons to renounce such desires in the future. To accomplish their purpose, they gradually created and inculcated man's first significant cultural achievement, the most primitive form of religion known as totemism.[9]

In totemism, as Freud understood it, there were two more or less universally observed commands. The first was not to marry within the totem clan and violate the incest taboo. The second was not to kill the totem animal worshipped by the clan members as a mythological ancestor-protector.[10] In this way, Freud theorized, the primal father's memory was unconsciously transferred to some appropriate totem animal which symbolized his destructive-protective power.[11] In this symbolic disguise, his feared memory could be honored, his prohibition against incest obeyed, and his longed-for protection invoked.

This symbolic substitution of some animal form for the father is quite understandable, according to Freud, since primal man thought of animals (as small children still do) in human terms.[12] Since many animals are equal or superior to man physically, primal man initially projected[13] his own inner state onto animals and naively experienced them as possessing mental powers equal and even superior to his own. Only with the passage of time and increased experience did primitive man come to realize that the psychological powers of animals were inferior to his own. Thereafter, the worship of totem animals and gods in half-animal form was replaced gradually by the worship of gods in human form and, finally, by the worship of only one God called the almighty Father.[14]

Freud based his totemistic theory about the origins of

religion and culture on Darwin's theory of the primal horde.[15] Many anthropologists, from the time of Malinowski's classic rebuttal[16] onwards, have pointed out a number of serious objections that stand in the way of a literal acceptance of Freud's theory. Freud himself thought that the primal struggle which he postulated must have occurred repeatedly over a lengthy period and not merely one time.[17] He acknowledged that the historical evidence available was inconclusive[18] but insisted that, even though we may not be able to demonstrate that the father of the primal horde was in fact *physically* attacked and murdered by his sons at some past time, the psychological equivalent of this hypothetical event takes place regularly in *fantasy* in connection with childhood experience of the Oedipus complex.[19] For, although in reality the small and helpless child is unable to fully vent his hostility against his rival father, in fantasy he is able to do so; there he can engage in feats of omnipotence and successfully imagine the way in which he would like to strike out against and eliminate his father.

Since the difference between fantasy and reality is still quite ambiguous in the mental life of a child, he can feel as guilty about something perpetrated in fantasy as he would had he done so in reality.[20] Hence, Freud concluded, whether or not the sons actually destroyed the primal father in reality, they certainly did (and still do) in fantasy; either way, they would have experienced the guilt and anxiety that led them to create the earliest form of religion and morality.[21]

The child who engages in aggressive Oedipal imaginings realizes in time that, although he may be able to best his father in fantasy, he cannot do so extramentally. Accordingly, he renounces his guilt-causing fantasies and yields to the requirements of the father's power and authority. In order to restrain and guide his desires, the child begins to introject his father's commands and attitudes with new seriousness, thereby hoping to avoid his father's punitive wrath and enjoy his approval and protection. This internalizing of paternal commands and attitudes marks the beginning of superego formation in the child and eventually results in a developed sense of moral obligation, or conscience, the shaping of which has been one of the chief concerns of religion throughout history.[22]

The Oedipal origin of conscience in childhood is the key, Freud thought, to understanding the origin and nature of the traditional commandments which religion claims to have received from God. Such commandments are, in reality, the traditional attitudes and dictates of human parents and other authority figures which have been introjected by repeated social conditioning and retained as deeply entrenched standards of the superego.[23]

Later on, according to Freud, the child grows up, becomes basically self-sufficient, and realizes the actual limitations of his father. But even though he has reached physical manhood, he still finds himself surrounded by powerful forces in nature which sometime seem hostile and threatening. In an anxious effort to understand and cope with such forces, primitive man intuitively recognized an analogy between the threatening and protective power of the unconsciously remembered father and the ambivalent power present in nature, which also seemed to threaten and punish as well as provide and protect. Accordingly, he personified the powerful forces in nature and, in an effort to influence them favorably, tried to relate to them as a child does to his father.[24] To this end he unconsciously projected[25] the powerful father image of childhood experience onto the mighty forces of nature and thought of them as God the almighty Father:

> Even the grown man, though he may know that he possesses greater strength, and though he has greater insight into the dangers of life, rightly feels that fundamentally he is just as helpless and unprotected as he

was in childhood and that in relation to the external world he is still a child. Even now, therefore, he cannot give up the protection which he enjoyed as a child. . . . He therefore looks back to the memory-image of the overrated father of his childhood, exalts it into a Deity, and brings it into the present and into reality. The emotional strength of this memory-image and the lasting nature of his need for protection are the two supports of his belief in God.[26]

## II.

Given Freud's understanding of the origin and meaning of the idea of God, it followed for him that religious beliefs are nothing more than unrealistic wishes stemming from unconsciously retained childhood attitudes. By means of religious beliefs (myths) and practices (rituals), man tries to protect himself, in an infantile way, from his fear of whatever threatens him with nonexistence.[27]

The most important of the mysterious evils which man experiences as threatening his existence is death. Primitive man found death a terrifying problem, since he was convinced that he should not have to die[28] and that death happened to others only as a result of violence or magic.[29]

This attitude is characteristic of primitive man given the naive and childlike state of his experience. Children initially have no knowledge of death or its necessity; until they learn about their mortality they assume that their existence will be unending.

With the passage of time and increased experience, historical man has arrived at the point where he reluctantly concedes the inevitability of biological death but persists in denying that death is the termination of his existence by inventing and believing in various myths of salvation which assure him that he is able to survive death.[30]

For all of the foregoing reasons, Freud concluded that

religious beliefs are *illusions* unconsciously manufactured in the service of infantile wish fulfillment, especially the desire to avoid facing the finality of death.[31] It should be noted, however, that when Freud referred to religious beliefs as illusions he departed from the usual meaning of the word and defined it in a way peculiarly his own:[32]

> When I say that these things are illusions, I must define the meaning of the word. An illusion is not the same thing as an error; nor is it necessarily an error. . . . It was an illusion of Columbus's that he had discovered a new sea route to the Indies. The part played by his wish in this error is very clear. . . . What is characteristic of illusions is that they are derived from human wishes. . . . Illusions need not be necessarily false – that is to say, unrealizable or in contradiction to reality. For instance, a middle class girl may have the illusion that a prince will come and marry her. This is possible; and a few such cases have occurred. That the Messiah will come and found a golden age is much less likely. Whether one classifies this belief as an illusion or as something analogous to a delusion will depend on ones's personal attitude. . . .
>
> Having thus taken our bearings, let us return once more to the question of religious doctrines. We can now repeat that all of them are illusions and insusceptible of proof. . . . [33]

An illusion was understood by Freud as an improbable possiblity. He did not deny that what he called an illusion is possible, but he thought of it as highly improbable because empirical indications that the possibility in question can actually exist outside the mind (apart from the projective mechanism of wish fulfillment) are either lacking or insufficient.

Freud personally believed that life after death is not

probable and that a realistic examination of the facts compels a mature human being to accept the stern demands of necessity with resignation and courage.[34] Later in his career, Freud changed his earlier opinion that "no instinct we possess is ready for a belief in death"[35] and advanced his melancholy theory of the death instinct which concluded that "the aim of all life is death."[36]

Since man has evolved from inorganic elements, he bears within himself the unconscious tendency to return to the state of quiescence or homeostatic freedom from tension that characterizes the inorganic realm.[37] Only then will he be free from the painful frustrations which always to some degree, but increasingly with age, characterize human existence.[38]

### III.

Organized religion was viewed by Freud as a kind of mass neurosis designed to achieve two results: First, it equips its practitioners with a belief-system that defends them from their fear of life's threatening dangers, especially death. Second, it provides a form of social indoctrination (encouraged by those in possession of political and economic power) that induces the masses to submit to exploitation (and frustration of instinctual desires) in exchange for the hope of eventual justice and happiness in the "next" life.[39]

Although Freud vigorously denied that his psychoanalytic theories were indebted to the thought of any philosopher, his understanding of religion as a kind of ideology that abets social oppression was probably influenced by Karl Marx. We know that Freud was acquainted with the ideas of Marx, at least in a general way, because he discussed some of them explicitly in his *New Introductory Lectures in Psychoanalysis.*[40]

Since for Freud religion stems from infantile fears and desires manipulated by parental and societal authority, it is necessarily neurotic, but with an important difference. The devotees of religion participate in a mass neurosis that spares them from the necessity of constructing a personal neurosis; this is why so many of them are apparently free from neurotic symptoms. Religion provides them with beliefs and practices which enable them to allay the anxiety and frustration deriving from their dread of death and the socially determined repression of their instinctual desires.[41]

Nonbelievers have no such remedies available and have to deal with these problems in other ways. Those who are not successful in adjusting to the demands of reality succumb to various forms of neurotic illness from which believers are spared.[42] In the long run, however, Freud was convinced that believers pay an unacceptable price for the apparent relief from neurotic anxiety and guilt afforded them by religion; they remain fixated in a state of infantile submission to repressive and growth-inhibiting forms of authority in exchange for illusory hopes.[43]

The real hope for mankind, as Freud saw it, is that gradually the realistic viewpoint of science will prevail and wean the masses from their superstitious religious beliefs.[44] When this goal has been achieved:

> They will, it is true, find themselves in a difficult situation. They will have to admit to themselves the full extent of their helplessness and their insignificance in the machinery of the universe; they can no longer be the object of tender care on the part of a beneficent Providence. They will be in the same position as a child who has left the parental house where he was so warm and comfortable. But surely infantilism is destined to be surmounted. Men cannot remain children forever; they must in the end go out into 'hostile life'....
>
> And, as for the great necessities of Fate, against which there is no help, they will learn to endure them

9

with resignation.[45]

## NOTES

1. *The Standard Edition of the Complete Works of Sigmund Freud*, ed. by James Strachey (London: Hogarth Press, 1966), XV 203-208, 210; IV, 255-265 (referred to hereafter as SE).

2. *Ibid.*, XX, 212-213

3. *Ibid.*, XV, 207-208

4. *Ibid.*, XIII, 156.

5. *Ibid.*, XVIII, 105-106; XIX, 31-32.

6. *Ibid.*, XIII, 50, 126-130; XX, 105-106.

7. *Ibid.*, XVIII, 78 n. 2; XXIII, 134.

8. *Ibid.*, XIII, 128-129; XIX, 73-74

9. *Ibid.*, XIII, 141-144; XXIII, 130-131.

10. *Ibid.*, XIII, 101-105.

11. *Ibid.*, XIII, 24-25, 127-128.

12. *Ibid.*, XIII, 76-77, 126-127.

13. *Ibid.*, XIII, 64.

14. *Ibid.*, XIII, 148-149; XXIII, 133-134.

15. *Ibid.*, XIII, 125-126; XXIII, 81-90; XX, 67-69.

16. Bronislaw Malinowski, *Sex and Repression in Savage Society* (New York: Harcourt Brace & Co., 1927).

17. SE XXIII, 82; XIII, 158, 142 n. 1.

18. *Ibid.*, XIII, 157-158.

19. *Ibid.*, XIII, 159-160. For the view of an anthropologist who agrees with Freud's interpretation of the psychological side of this matter, see Alfred L. Kroeber, "Totem and Taboo in Retrospect," in *The American Journal of Sociology*, 45 (1939), 446.

20. SE XIII, 85-90.

21. *Ibid.*, XIII, 157-161.

22. *Ibid.*, XXII, 164.

23. *Ibid.*, XIX, 36-37. The Freudian superego does not correspond exactly to the traditional notion of conscience. The superego encompasses a positive side, the ego ideal, and a negative

10

side, the conscience. The ego ideal includes all of the positive attitudes and standards that a person has been taught to identify with and emulate. The Freudian conscience represents only negative and forbidden kinds of behavior which one has been conditioned to avoid as dangerous and shameful.

24. *Ibid.*, XXI, 24.

25. *Ibid.*, XIII, 64. Tillich noted that explaining away religious belief as mere psychological projection did not originate with Freud. Ludwig Feuerbach had already suggested the idea in his criticism of Hegel's philosophy of religion. See Feuerbach's *The Essence of Christianity* (London: Trubner and Co., 1881), 1-31. Karl Marx carried Feuerbach's theory a step farther by asserting that the suffering caused by socio-economic exploitation is what motivates man to project a heavenly realm where present injustices will finally be redressed. See his *Critique of Hegel's Philosophy of Right* (Cambridge: Cambridge University Press, 1970), 131. The idea that projection is involved in religious ideas is older, however, than Feuerbach. The Greek Philosopher Xenophanes employed the notion of projection to criticize the immoral behavior of the gods described in the Homeric myths. See Paul Tillich, *Perspectives on 19th and 20th Century Protestant Theology,* ed. by Carl E. Bratten (New York: Harper & Row Publishers, Inc., 1967), 139-141. For a clear exposition of Xenophanes' understanding of projection, see Cornelius Loew, *Myth, Sacred History, and Philosophy* (New York: Harcourt, Brace and World, Inc., 1967), 211-213.

26. SE XXII, 163.

27. *Ibid.*, XIII, 78-81; XXI, 18-19.

28. *Ibid.*, XIV, 296.

29. *Ibid.*, XIII, 59; XIV, 292-297; XVIII, 45.

30. *Ibid.*,XXI, 19, 33-35.

31. *Ibid.*, XXI, 30-33.

32. Ernest Jones, *The Life and Work of Sigmund Freud,* 3 vols. (New York: Basic Books, Inc., 1953-1957), III, 356.

33. SE XXI, 30-31.

34. *Ibid.*, XVIII, 44-45; XXI, 50, 54.

35. *Ibid.*, XIV, 296.

36. *Ibid.*, XVIII, 38-40, 44-45.

37. *Ibid.*, XVIII, 36-40; XIX, 40.

38. Jones, *The Life and Work of Sigmund Freud,* III, 276-280.
39. SE XXI, 1-29.
40. *Ibid.,* XXII, 176-181.
41. *Ibid.,* XXI, 37-39; 81, 84-85.
42. *Ibid.,* XXI, 44, 85; XI, 123
43. *Ibid.,* XVIII, 141-142.
44. *Ibid.,* XXI, 51-56.
45. *Ibid.,* XXI, 50.

*CHAPTER TWO*

# Tillich's Response to Freud's Existentialism

### I.

FREUDIAN PSYCHOANALYSIS WAS VIEWED BY Tillich as an important part of the *existentialist* movement of the twentieth century. Consequently, some consideration should be given to Tillich's understanding of existentialism in order to better grasp his interpretation of psychoanalysis.[1]

Tillich regarded existentialism as a movement of protest against the "philosophy of consciousness," by which he meant the philosophical tradition that began with the rationalism of Descartes in the seventeenth century and reached its apogee with Hegel's idealism in the nineteenth century. This tradition construed man in terms of intellect as opposed to will and the unconscious or nonrational elements in human nature. Such Appollonian emphasis eventually precipitated a Dionysian reaction.

The abstract, intellectualizing philosophy of Descartes was opposed from its outset by Pascal's philosophy of the heart. But it was not until the middle of the nineteenth century, when Hegel's all-encompassing system seemed to have triumphed, that protest began to erupt with full intensity. Tillich saw the reaction against Hegelianism beginning with the late thought of Schelling, who was followed by Kierkegaard, Marx, Hartman, and Schopenhauer. The protest was then taken up by the "life" philosophers, Nietzsche, Dilthey, and Bergson. After World War I, the movement was continued by the German existentialists, Heidegger and Jaspers, and after World War II by Sartre (Heidegger's former student) and others.

All of these men objected in their various ways (against the philosophy of consciousness) that human existence should not be described with abstract theoretical concepts taken from the purely logical order but rather in terms derived from concrete experience of human *existence*. They agreed that essentialist interpretations of human nature (which define man from the standpoint of ideal possibilities) should be rejected, especially Hegel's claim that the estranged and conflictual elements of existence had been reconciled by his system. Human existence, they demurred, remains a grim predicament in which man is continually beset by negativities which threaten him with nonbeing. An adequate interpretation of man, therefore, must acknowledge that he is characterized by anxious concern and the threat of self-loss.[2]

Although Tillich was sympathetic with the existentialist protest against essentialist distortions of reality, he was convinced that existentialism ultimately has no validity apart from essentialist notions (about the way things ought to be) which it tacitly presupposes.[3] Tillich also noted that, regardless of the professed atheism of some of the existentialist philosophers, there is nothing inherently atheistic (or theistic) about the existentialist analysis of the human predicament as long as it remains just that. Whenever existentialist philosophers go beyond analyzing their experience of the human predicament and provide answers to the ultimate questions raised by that predicament, their answers are derived from some religious or quasi-religious tradition, and not from their analysis of existence.[4]

## II.

In Tillich's judgment, the existentialist analysis of the human predicament is in essential agreement with the classical Christian interpretation of man. The Judeo-Christian tradition always has been profoundly aware of the irrational and destructive forces that threaten man's tenuous existence. This tradition found initial written expression in the oldest of the two creation accounts in the book of Genesis (2:4b-3:24), which attempts to account for the evils (sin, tragedy, suffering, and death) which have afflicted man throughout his history. It then underwent a dramatic eschatological development in the Jewish apocalyptic theology[5] of the late post-exilic period; from there it was carried over into the Christian interpretation of existence found in the New Testament.

If the Judeo-Christian understanding of the evils which threaten man is compared with the analysis of the human predicament provided by existentialist philosophers, the two, Tillich thought, manifest striking similarities. The biblical view represents a venerable tradition reaching far into the historical past, employing symbolic religious language (myth). The existentialist analysis is contemporary and uses the abstract categories of philosophy. Both viewpoints, however, are concerned with the negativities that have disrupted human existence from time immemorial.

It was Tillich's opinion that this common concern with the problem of existence makes existentialism the natural ally of Christianity. Existentialism has presented contemporary man with an uncompromisingly honest analysis of the human situation. And it is the recognition of the tragic nature of his situation that drives man to ask the ultimate questions for which the Christian message provides the definitive answer.[6]

For Tillich, the crucified and risen Jesus is God's definitive answer to tragedy, injustice, and every other form of evil that can threaten man with nonbeing and tempt him to discouragement and despair. But man is not able to recognize the cogency of the answer until he is brought to full awareness of his predicament and *personally experiences* a need for the answer. And that is precisely the task which existentialism has facilitated in presenting contemporary man with an unflinching description of his existence. This analysis would not have the same force if it had been offered to man from the hands of religion. Existentialism is, therefore, an invaluable contemporary aid in proclaiming the Christian message in a way that enhances its comprehensibility as definitive answer.[8]

## III.

When Freudian psychoanalysis, with its central postulate of the unconscious, made its appearance at the beginning of the twentieth century (the *Interpretation of Dreams* was published in 1900), it joined forces with existentialism and became part of the movement of protest against the philosophy of consciousness. Psychoanalysis was influenced by the current existentialist mood and, in turn, contributed significantly to that mood by its own penetrating analysis of the unconscious and irrational forces that contribute to the human experience of estrangement and tragic suffering.[9] Psychoanalysis also provided a scientific foundation for some of the insights that existentialist philosophers and artists had arrived at through intuition.[10]

There is, however, a basic difference between the viewpoints of psychoanalysis and existentialist philosophy. Existentialism considers the human situation as one in which anxiety and suffering are *universally* experienced because of negativities which truly and inescapably threaten man's finite existence. Depth psychology, on the other hand, directs its attention to the ways in which *some* men try to escape from imagined or exaggerated negativities by fleeing into the unreality of neurosis or psychosis.[11]

Some psychoanalysts deny the distinction between *existential* and *neurotic* anxiety and claim they can free a man from the former as well as the latter. Tillich, however, thought that such psychoanalysts should accept the analysis of finitude provided by the existentialists. This analysis shows that man necessarily experiences "existential" anxiety, because he realizes, clearly or obscurely, that everything finite comes from nothing and returns to nothing and that, consequently, his own finite existence is truly threatened by nonbeing. Neurotic structures can be removed by psychotherapy, but the structures of finitude cannot.[12]

Christian theology sides with existential philosophy in this matter and maintains that psychoanalysis cannot heal man of his basic or existential anxiety. The structures of finitude which underlie man's basic anxiety require not a psychotherapeutic healing in time and space but a divinely bestowed gift of healing *acceptance* which assures man that ultimately he is able to transcend the evils within time and space that threaten him with loss of his personal being and meaning.[13]

The analyst can become the instrument of such transcendent assurance (as can other supporting and accepting friends) for the experience of his acceptance enables the one being accepted to understand and believe in that transcendent acceptance which promises to ultimately save man from his dread of nonbeing—the acceptance which is offered to man by God in the experience of grace. Since God is the infinite power of being who alone is able to overcome nonbeing, it follows that he alone is able to supply the assurance which can free finite man from his basic anxiety in the face of nonbeing. It is when man experiences himself as loved and accepted by (therefore forgiven by) God that he becomes essentially free from his anxiety-causing fear of losing his being and meaning forever (as possible punishment or meaningless destiny.)[14]

## IV.

Tillich considered Freud's interpretation of the ills which afflict the human psyche to be a valuable addition to the existentialist analysis of man's predicament. Psychoanalysis, along with existentialism in general, has helped Christian theology rediscover many existentialist elements in its own tradition which had been minimized or forgotten under the influence of the philosophy of consciousness.

For example, psychoanalysis has provided theology with a deeper insight into such traditional religious concepts as sin (infantile regression resulting in self-estrangement), the demonic (the destructive, irrational demands of the unconscious), grace (healing acceptance), the neurotic distortions possible in perfectionistic morality (compensatory exhibitionism),[15] and the psychological factors involved in the creation of religious symbols.[16]

Although Tillich found much to commend in Freud's psychological observations about human nature, he also found it necessary to fault some of Freud's ideas because of the inadequate philosophical understanding of man on which they are based. Freud arrived at a number of unduly pessimistic conclusions about human nature because he failed to recognize the important distinction between man's *essential* being (what it is really possible for man to become) and his *existential* being (what man actually is at the present time). Freudian anthropology envisions man only in his existential estrangement from himself and does not explicitly acknowledge man's capacity for actualizing his essential goodness.[17]

This negative perception of human nature led Freud, for example, to formulate a doctrine of libido which is deficient from the Christian point of view. Freud taught that man is infinite desire which can never be satisfied. When man finally realizes that he can never still the infinite craving of his libido, he longs unconsciously to return to the oblivion of the earlier evolutionary stage of inorganic quiescence to escape from his increasingly painful existence. Such a hopeless state of mind results in what Freud called the death wish.

Tillich thought that Freud's melancholy theory of frustrated libido driving man toward death can be accorded a measure of acceptance if man is considered solely from the viewpoint of existential estrangement. Christian theology agrees that man can be in a tragic state of alienation from his essential being. This is what traditional theology has called the state or condition of sin. Lacking any responsible controls or goals by which to limit and guide the potentially unlimited desires of his libido, estranged man can succumb to a weary despair that drives him suicidally to wish for death. But theology also knows that man can be considered from the viewpoint of his essential goodness and can be saved from his self-estrangement.

Man, Christianity insists, can be essentially freed from concupiscence by directing his vagrant libido to definite persons and goals through meaningful love and commitment. Such a course of action makes it possible for man to achieve real fulfillment in terms of his essential nature and frees him from the despair-causing unfulfillment of alienated desire. Freud's theory of libido and its concomitant death wish is correct as an analysis of uncommitted man in the state of existential estrangement. But it errs in failing to recognize man's capacity for achieving genuine fulfillment by actualizing his essential being.[18]

The distorted view of man proposed by Freud was probably encouraged by his profession, which required him to be preoccupied habitually with the pathological suffering of patients unable to achieve realistic fulfillment of their desires. Fortunately, in practice he mitigated his gloomy anthropology by proceeding therapeutically on the assumption that man can be encouraged to strive in the direction of health and free himself from psychopathic forms of estrangement. Man's essential being is implicitly acknowledged by Freud's assumption that the healthy and mature side of human nature is a real and better possibility that can be actualized with the help of psychotherapy.[19]

## NOTES

1. Paul Tillich, *Theology of Culture,* ed. by Robert C. Kimball (New York: Oxford University Press, 1964), 113.

2. *Ibid.,* 76-111, 116-117.

3. Paul Tillich, "Existentialism and Psychotherapy," in *Psychoanalysis and Existential Philosophy,* ed. by Hendrik M. Ruitenbeek (New York: E.P. Dutton & Co., Inc., 1962), 9.

4. Tillich, *Theology of Culture,* 125.

5. Not until the advent of apocalyptic theology in the book of Daniel (165 B.C.) did Jewish religious thought envision a future life of unending fulfillment beyond death as part of God's purpose for man. Cf. D.S. Russell, *The Method and Message of Jewish Apocalyptic* (Philadelphia: Westminster press, 1964), 353-374.

6. Paul Tillich, *Systematic Theology,* 3 vols. (Chicago: The University of Chicago Press, 1951-1963), I, 130.

7. *Ibid.,* II, 97-99; 118-135.

8. *Ibid.,* I, 61-66; II, 27-28.

9. Tillich, "Existentialism and Psychotherapy," 1-10.

10. Tillich, *Theology of Culture,* 117.

11. *Ibid.,* 118.

12. Paul Tillich, *The Courage to Be* (New Haven, Connecticut: Yale University Press, 1952), 64-77; "Existentialism and Psychotherapy," 10-14. There seems to be evidence that Freud himself implicitly acknowledged the difference between neurotic and existential anxiety. See Harry M. Tiebout, Jr., "Freud and Existentialism," in the *Journal of Nervous and Mental Diseases,* 126, April, 1958, 341-352; Loomis, "The Psychiatric Legacy of

Paul Tillich," 92.

13. Tillich, *Systematic Theology*, I, 191-192; III, 281.

14. Tillich, *Theology of Culture*, 118-119, 122; *Courage to Be*, 155-186.

15. Tillich, *Theology of Culture*, 123-124; *Systematic Theology*, III, 240.

16. Paul Tillich, "The Religious Symbol," in *Religious Experience and Truth*, ed. by Sidney Hook (New York: New York University Press, 1961), 304-306.

17. Tillich, *Theology of Culture*, 119-120. For a detailed explanation of Tillich's distinction between man's essential and existential being, see his *Systematic Theology*, I, 202-204.

18. Tillich, *Theology of Culture*, 119-120; *Systematic Theology*, II, 53-55.

19. Tillich, *Theology of Culture*, 120.

# CHAPTER THREE

# Tillich's Response
# To Freud's Scientism

## I.

SOME OF THE MATERIAL IN THIS CHAPTER, ESPE-
cially the second through the fifth of its nine divisions, is
quite abstract and technical. Nevertheless, it is essential to
an adequate grasp of Tillich's evaluation of Freud. Those
who persevere will be rewarded when it is time to harvest
the insights provided by Tillich in chapters IV and V.

Tillich emphatically rejected the dogmatic scientism
which led Freud to assert that only scientific methodology
provides man with genuine truth about reality. Freud con-
tended that:

> It is inadmissible to declare that science is one field of
> human intellectual activity, and that religion and
> philosophy are others, at least as valuable, and that
> science has no business to interfere with the other two,
> that they all have an equal claim to truth, and that
> everyone is free to choose whence he shall draw his
> belief. Such an attitude is considered particularly
> respectable, tolerant, broad-minded, and free from nar-
> row prejudices. Unfortunately, it is not tenable. . . .

truth cannot be tolerant and cannot admit compromise or limitations. ... scientific research looks on the whole field of human activity as its own, and must adopt an uncompromisingly critical attitude towards any other power that seeks to usurp any part of its province.[1]

To this position Tillich responded that the use of broader philosophical reasoning is not only permissable but imperative if man is to arrive at adequate answers to the ulitmate questions that arise from his experience of a finite and contingent world. Man is reponsible for providing answers to his ultimate as well as preliminary questions; a truly adequate approach to understanding reality enables him to deal with both.[2]

In Tillich's world view, the human experience of finitude was fundamental.[3] It is man's anxious realization that he and everything in his world are finite — come from nothing and return to nothing — that drives him to raise philosophical questions about the mystery of being. What is being? How was contingent being able to emerge from nonbeing? Ultimately, why is there something rather than nothing?[5] All of these questions are bound to be of concern to man because they ask about that on which his own being or notbeing ultimately depends.[6]

Tillich thought that if man is fully open to the implications of his finitude, he is driven to the recognition of being-itself, the dimension of infinite and eternal being which is logically prior to all finite being and, consequently, its ultimate ground.[7] For Tillich, being-itself is a philosophical way of speaking of God; therefore, "God is the answer to the question implied in man's finitude; he is the name for that which concerns man ultimately."[8]

The positivistic bias in Freud's narrower understanding of truth would invalidate all ultimate questions and anwers because they are beyond the pale of empirical methodology.

Nevertheless, Tillich affirmed, man has an obligation to ask and answer such questions, for he bears within himself the power of self-transcendence. This power manifests itself as reason and freedom of choice and enables man to creatively hypothesize beyond the limits of the immediately given. Because he is capable of self-transcendence (is able to transcend indefinitely the limits of what he presently is and knows), man is able to wonder and voice the questions implicit in his perception of facts. It is precisely such transempirical probing that leads to the hypothesizing which underlies all human progress, including scientific progress.

Man has a duty to engage in such hypothesizing (tentative problem solving) for he realizes that in virtue of his reason and freedom of choice he is responsible for what he is and becomes; he must try to foresee and circumvent the negativities that threaten his fragile existence with nonbeing. Creative anticipation of the future is universally incumbent on man.

And if it is reasonable and necessary for man to hypothesize about the probable answers to questions of *preliminary* concern, then it is also necessary to do the same with questions of *ultimate* concern. The power of self-transcending reason obliges man to seek a better understanding of the unconditional mystery on which his own being or not-being ultimately depends.[9]

It is misguided and impermissible, therefore, to insist, as Freud did, that man has no right to take ultimate questions seriously: "The question of God *must* be asked because the threat of nonbeing, which man experiences as anxiety, drives him to the question of being conquering nonbeing and of courage conquering anxiety."[10]

## II.

When analyzing the human ability to grasp the truth, Tillich distinguished what he called *ontological* (philosophic) reason from *technical* (scientific) reason. He regarded ontological reason as the more comprehensive of the two and considered technical reason to be an instrument in its service.

By "ontological" reason Tillich meant the cognitive approach to reality that seeks to understand the implications of "being"[11] in all of its various dimensions — cognitive, aesthetic, practical, *and* technical. Technical reason, on the other hand, is concerned only with cognitive acts that deal with the empirical discovery of means to ends; it regards all broader cognitive and noncognitive functions in human experience as alien to reason.

The primary task of ontological reason is to search out the ends, values, and norms which guide man's choice of means; only after determining ends does it concern itself with the problem of means. It is then that technical "reasoning" may be employed appropriately by reason in the broader sense. Technical "reasoning" has an important contribution to make to the integral functioning of reason, but this contribution can be fully adequate only when guided by ontological reason. The norms and values that technical reason tacitly presupposes are received from some other source, and, by its own admission, it is unable to deal with questions of ultimate value and meaning.

The broad ontological understanding of reason was regarded by Tillich as predominant in the philosophical tradition of the West from the time of Parmenides (c. 500 BC) to the time of Hegel (c. 1800 AD). But due to the influence of English empiricism and the failure of German idealism to answer adequately the questions raised by empiricism, the narrow technical approach to reason has gradually gained ascendance. Since the emergence of scientific positivism in the middle of the nineteenth century, with its distorted emphasis on the exclusive prerogatives of empirical methodology, there has been a danger that technical "reasoning" might separate itself completely from reason in the more inclusive sense (Freud is clearly an example of this tendency).

The pervasive influence of technical reason in the modern world has led to widespread neglect of ontological reason and encouraged the attitude that man has no right to utilize the important transempirical indications in his experience which can help him discover the aims, norms, and values necessary for achieving authentic existence.[12] This unhappy development has led to a spiritual vacuum in Western culture (reflected in the negativity of much modern art); this vacuum is constantly in danger of being filled by irrational and destructive forces (like Nazism), since eventually norms and values have to come from somewhere.

## III.

The undue emphasis placed upon technical reason in modern times has resulted in the baneful overemphasis of a cognitive stance which Tillich called *controlling knowledge.* By controlling knowledge, he meant the approach to knowing reality that deliberately strives to maintain psychic distance and methodological detachment in the relationship between knowing subject and known object (the methodology of the natural sciences).

The polar elements of *union* and *detachment* are necessarily present to some degree in every act of knowing, but the controlling knowledge characteristic of the natural sciences tries to eliminate the element of union between knower and known while emphasizing the element of detachment. It deliberately tries to achieve an objectivity which is free from distorting subjective elements. To accomplish this, controlling knowledge has to ignore the unique subjective qualities present in existing things and must regard them distantly as calculable objects to be manipulated within a means-to-end relationship.

It was readily granted by Tillich that the use of controlling knowledge is sometimes desirable and necessary. But it is not the only way to arrive at knowledge. In fact, there are situations where controlling knowledge is the least adequate way of doing so. The more complex the reality being considered, the more manifoldly it participates in the life process, the less adequate controlling knowledge becomes to inclusively know and understand that reality. This is especially true where man is concerned:

> While the nature of metals admits of an overwhelming amount of objectifying knowledge and technical use, the nature of man does not. Man resists objectification, and if his resistance to it is broken, man himself is broken. A truly objective relation to man is determined by the element of union; the element of detachment is secondary. It is not absent; there are levels in man's bodily, psychic and mental constitution which can and must be grasped by controlling knowledge. But this is neither the way of knowing human nature nor is it the way of knowing any individual personality in past or present, including one's self[13]

Controlling knowledge artificially separates a thing from the total life process which that thing either embodies or in which it participates. Life processes are characterized by totality, spontaneity, and uniqueness; it is the unexpected which can well up from the subtle randomness present in the heart of matter that leads to the new. An experiment, however, presupposes the isolation of some particular element from the total life process and the methodical elimination of all but its general characteristics which can be observed with regularity under controlled conditions. By reason of its self-imposed limitations, many experienceable aspects of being are deliberately ignored by controlling knowledge. Consequently, Tillich concluded, an additional approach to knowledge is required to arrive at a truly adequate understanding of reality. There is such an approach, and it is called *receiving knowledge.*

Receiving knowledge is existential knowledge in the sense of involving man through *experiential participation,* especially emotional participation, with all possible levels of whatever he is knowing. Positive emotional participation facilitates union and precludes the projection of distorting presuppositions which prevent a thing from being known in its totality and uniqueness.

This more intimate and comprehensive knowledge by intuitive participation is possible for man, Tillich explained, because nothing that man encounters within the self-world structure of reality is completely foreign to him. There are structural elements in his own being which all other beings participate in to some degree. Therefore, that which initially seems strange can eventually become familiar by reason of discovered elements of self-relatedness.[14]

## IV.

It is, above all, the religious experience of unconditional mystery that the restrictive presuppositions of controlling knowledge are unable to deal with adequately. Concern with a dimension of reality experienced as infinitely transcending the subject-object structure of empirical experience is obviously beyond the self-imposed limits of controlling knowledge. Neither the subjective pole of ultimate concern nor the transobjective pole of that which unconditionally transcends all objects is able to be dealt with by empirical methodology. *Receiving* knowledge, however, is able (indirectly) to experience transcendent reality and give inferential expression to its implications.

Through the fuller cognitive union of receiving knowledge man can enter into sympathetic communion with beings that participate with him in the mystery of being and arrive at an intuitive recognition of their meaning and the way he should relate to them within the total life process. If man can arrive at an analogical understanding of those things which *he transcends* within the life process, he can also come to an analogous understanding of the unconditional mystery which he experiences as *transcending himself* and the total life process. It is in this infinite power of being (being-itself) that man and all other finite beings ultimately participate, and this participation is the basis of man's ability to understand analogically something of the transcendent reality which grounds the universe.[15]

## V.

It is clear, then, that Freud's insistence that truth can be verified only in an experimental way was dismissed by Tillich as mistaken. Tillich did acknowledge, however, that there is an important element of truth in Freud's position: All reasonable statements must be verifiable in some way. But *experimental* verification is not the only way to achieve that end. Reasonable interpretations can and must be provided for those indirectly experienceable (inferable) realities that transcend the empirical. Such interpretations must also be measured against some verifying standard of judgment.

To accomplish this task, a broader criterion must be appealed to within the life process itself, and that criterion is *experience.* Man is able to consult all his past learning experiences stored in memory. This fund of memories includes many verifying experiences of a nonexperimental kind. Man's ability to intuitively scan all past learning experiences in a rapid nondiscursive way (dispensing with time-consuming verbalization) gives him ready access to pertinent memories that enable him to interpret his transempirical experience analogically. Through intuitive recognition man is able to discern those elements in his past experience that possess analogical complementarity with obscurely known elements being considered in his present experience.

Therefore, if man is trying to discover what the unknown cause of some effect might be like and remembers a similar effect for which he *does* know the cause, he may reasonably infer that since the two effects are similar something about their causes is probably also similar. Consequently, he may reasonably use the known cause as a model which to some degree approximates the unkown cause.

Because of its indirect nature, *experiential* verification imparts a relative kind of certitude possessing various degrees of probability; it cannot give the absolute certitude yielded by empirical immediacy. The indirect kind of verification which appeals to the total range of human experience, and not merely objective data, is always somewhat obscure and subject to subsequent revision within the life process. Clarifications inevitably occur with the passage of time and increased experience and involve a dialectic in which earlier assumptions are questioned and revised in the light of later discoveries. Thus the life process itself eventually corrects the provisional conclusions arrived at under the aegis of experiential verification.

The knowledge derived from experiential verification is less exact and certain than that derived from repeatable experiments, but is is truer to life and one need not disrupt the life process to obtain it. Furthermore, it is the only possible means of judging those aspects of reality beyond the range of empirical scrutiny.[16]

Tilllich acknowledged that natural science provides man with important truth; but the kind of truth it can talk about with competence is, by definition, restricted to the surface of man's experience. Its limited methodology allows it to say nothing about the unconditional ground of all being encountered in the depths of human experience. There is need, therefore, for both kinds of knowledge, scientific *and* philosophic. For, although scientific knowledge is empirically certain, it is not ultimately significant.[17]

## VI.

On the other hand, Tillich allowed that philosophical knowledge also has its limits and agreed with Freud that the genuineness of one's belief in God is not something that can be proven or demonstrated rationally with compelling certitude. Tillich was of the unusual opinion (inherited from Kierkegaard) that to speak of God's "existence" suggests that God is a finite being like other finite beings which "stand out" of nonbeing by virtue of some ultimate creative principle. That, however, is absurd, Tillich concluded, since God is being-itself, or the creative ground of every essence *and* existence. As such, God necessarily transcends existence.[18] (Since Tillich allowed other general concepts to be employed analogically when speaking of God, many have accused him of being arbitrary and inconsistent for refusing to allow "existence" also to be predicated of God.)[19]

In addition, only something finite which can become an object of sensory perception for some experiencing subject can be "proven" or demonstrated with empirical certainty. The reality of the divine ground transcends the subject-object structure of empirical experience and is necessarily prior to every finite thing within it. Therefore, to speak of "proving" god's existence (in the modern sense of that term) is illogical and indicates a failure to understand correctly the unconditional mystery signified by the word "God"[20]

The fact that many find the traditional "proofs" for the existence of God unconvincing indicates that such proofs have convincing power only for those predisposed by personal experience of the unconditional and a special intellectual bent. Nevertheless, even though the traditional proofs do not succeed in "proving" anything, they are still significant indications of the human experience of the *question* of God.

It is man's experience of unconditional mystery that

drives him to ask the question of God, and this question requires an answer. Any positive answer given, however, cannot be proven but is *believed* on the basis of the prior experience of the unconditional which prompted both the question and the search for its answer. Efforts at proving God's existence are really attempts to answer questions about the mysterious reality of God already experienced in the encounter of faith.[21]

## VII.

For Tillich, faith experience is always in some measure revelatory, and, contrary to Freud, he thought that, correctly understood, divine revelation can be a genuine source of human knowledge.

Human efforts to understand the meaning of revelation should distinguish carefully between God's self-manifestation as the unconditional ground of all being and the historically limited way in which the human recipient of such experience will attempt to articulate its implications. Revelatory experience does not involve the verbal dictation of information about God or temporal events; nor should any of the paradigms for revelatory communication used by precritical ages be taken literally. Mythological descriptions of revelation should be understood as symbolic expressions of man's experience that unconditional mystery has manifested itself to him:

> Revelation of that which is essentially and necessarily mysterious means the manifestation of something within the context of ordinary experience which transcends the ordinary context of experience. Something more is known of the mystery after its has become manifest in revelation. First, its reality has become a matter of experience. Second, our relation to it has become a matter of experience. Both of these are

cognitive elements. But revelation does not dissolve the mystery into knowledge. Nor does it add anything directly to the totality of our ordinary knowledge, namely to our knowledge about the subject-object structure of reality.[22]

What God manifests in revelatory experience is *himself* as transcendent mystery, not verbal propositions about himself. The human recipient of such experience is able to articulate the insights it has suggested about the divine-human relationship, but he can never clearly or fully articulate the mysterious nature of the unconditional itself. Furthermore, the revelatory insights that he can articulate are expressed with historically limited explanatory models available within his culture. Consequently, inspired statements about the divine-human relationship are subject to qualification in the light of later developments in human understanding. Later ages will experience reality and the questions it raises differently than earlier ages; they will express the implications of revelatory experience with an awareness of new cognitive elements present in the way ultimate questions are being asked and answered.

The "verbal inspiration" sometimes generated by revelatory experience is not a kind of divine manipulation of human reason, Tillich cautioned. Rather, it is an ecstatic state of insight which results when the human mind is enabled to transcend the limitations which ordinarily restrict its range of knowing to the finite subject-object structure of reality.[23]

It is noteworthy that Tillich was in essential agreement with Freud's rejection of literally conceived mythological explanations of revelation.[24] As usual, however, Tilllich's agreement was dialectical. He said *yes* to Freud's rejection of outmoded paradigms for revelation, but *no* to Freud's assumption that religiously concerned man necessarily understands his belief in divine revelation with the scientifically inadequate assumptions of the unlettered man on the street: "We must ask every critic of theology to deal with theology with the same fairness which is demanded from everyone who deals, for instance, with physics—namely, to attack the most advanced and not some obsolete forms of a discipline."[25]

## VIII.

Tillich also agreed with Freud that claims made for the authority of sacred scripture which appeal to statements within scripture are obviously invalid. The Bible can be recognized and accepted as a book written under the influence of divine inspiration only by someone who has personally experienced the realities of faith pointed to by the words of scripture.[25] As to claims made for the authority of the Bible based on personal religious experience, Tillich concurred with Freud that such experience is a reasonable basis of belief only for its recipient; it has no verifying power where others are concerned. He also acknowledged that it is possible to confuse subjective states of mere emotion or overexcitement (sometimes artificially induced) with genuine religious experience. It is within the ecstatic (charismatic) movements that this danger is particularly present. It seemed probable to Tillich that within such movements this mistaken identification is succumbed to more often than not.[27]

But, while Freud asserted that all religious experience could be reduced to unconscious psychological factors, Tillich countered that genuine faith experience includes an *unconditional* element (or quality) that transcends finite psychological processes and descriptive categories. Even though revelatory experience has a psychological side, it involves a dimension of reality which transcends finite psychological powers.[28]

When asked how one is able to determine the genuineness of religious experience, Tillich answered that the unconditional element present in genuine faith experience cannot be artificially induced or manufactured by human efforts. The experience of the unconditional has the character of an unexpected and transcendently bestowed gift (the divine self-gift); finite man cannot demand it or grasp it with his own power but can only be open to being grasped by it.[29]

Also, genuine faith experience imparts a power which enables man to transcend himself creatively with new insight into reality and the demands of the present. False religious experience is a blinding form of self-elevation (not self-transcendence) which destructively (regressively) turns away from the present demands of reality.[30] In other words, "By their fruits you shall know them."

Tillich affirmed (in open sympathy with the objections of men like Freud) that genuine revelatory experience and the inspired understanding which can result from it are *never* irrational and do not produce anything that is absurd, illogical, or contrary to reason.[31] While in an ecstatic revelatory state, reason is aware of a dimension of reality that transcends its ordinary condition, but anything that reason understands as a result of such experience must be expressed with the concepts and logical structures already present within the ordinary experience of man. Reason's capacity for being carried beyond its ordinary condition in no way denies its ordinary condition.[32]

This means that man must employ language which derives from his ordinary experience of finite objects in order to communicate about the unconditional, even though he knows the unconditional infinitely transcends such object-determined language. Such language is used in a symbolically analogous way and should not be understood literally.[33]

## IX.

To speak about God in a symbolic manner is valid, Tillich concluded, because the power by which every finite thing in the universe is able to be what it is derives ultimately from the infinite power of the divine ground (being-itself). It follows from this that everything in the universe can be understood as a symbol which points beyond itself to the presence of the divine ground in whose power and meaning it participates and of which it is a finite manifestation.[34]

It would be impossible to speak about God without the use of symbols, Tillich maintained; moreover, "to say anything about God in the literal sense of the words used means to say something false about Him. The symbolic in relation to God is not less true than the literal, but it is the only true way of speaking about God."[35]

A symbol, as Tillich defined it, must be carefully distinguished from a sign. Both symbol and sign point beyond themselves to some other reality which they represent. But, while a sign can be arbitrarily chosen and has no necessary connection with that for which it stands, a symbol has an intrinsic connection with its referent, because it participates in its power and meaning; this experientially grounded participation is the basis of a symbol's efficacy.[35]

The critical juncture in the idea of God is between the experience of the unconditional and the concrete symbols by which man mediates to himself (and others) some understanding of the experienced unconditional. There is always a danger that the finite symbols used to refer to the unconditional will be taken literally and mistaken for the divine mystery itself, thereby implying that God is a finite being. The possibility of such misguided identification is part of the ambiguity that characterizes religion under the conditions of existence; human attempts to express the experience of infinite mystery with the poverty of finite

36

language regularly generate misunderstanding.

Accordingly, it should always be clearly indicated, Tillich remonstrated, that it is "the God above God" who is really God. By this he meant that when the word "God" is spoken, the primary referent intended should be the divine mystery which infinitely transcends the finite symbols that man has used historically to point to it.[37]

Because of the perennial human tendency to mistakenly identify the divine reality with its finite symbols, Tillich thought that a paradoxical kind of atheism, which says *no* to all superstitious and inadequate ways of speaking about ulitmate reality, will always accompany the advancing understanding of religion on its journey through history. Christianity itself was originally accused of this kind of atheism, and Tillich would not have been averse to the suggestion that Freud's atheism was largely of this kind.[38]

The ambiguity which characterizes religion under the conditions of existence serves as a reminder that the divine mystery which reveals itself in faith experience is not identical with religion even though it inspires and intends the creation of religion. Religion itself is not revealed.[39] It is created by man to express his understanding of the divine mystery which manifests itself to him in faith experience.[40] In other words, what God reveals is not religion but the mystery of his unconditional reality. Man's response to God's self-revelation is faith. And religion is the way that faith expresses symbolically in human community its understanding of the unconditional mystery by which it has been grasped.

As something humanly created (albeit divinely inspired and necessary), religion is finite, culturally conditioned, and historically limited. That means that its viewpoint is subject to the distorting obsolescence that overtakes all human efforts at expressing within time the meaning of eternal mystery. Religion, therefore, and all the symbols which it uses to point to the presence and meaning of the holy, must continually be reformed and may never claim for itself the absoluteness of the Absolute. For this reason, Tillich regarded the reasonable criticism of religion provided by Freud and others as something that should be positively valued by all who wish to understand more adequately the meaning of their religious tradition.[41]

## NOTES

1. Sigmund Freud, *New Introductory Lectures on Psychoanalysis,* translated by W.J.H. Spratt (New York: W.W. Norton, 1933), 219. This translation seems to reflect the mind of Freud more accurately than its counterpart in SE XXII, 160.

2. Paul Tillich, *Biblical Religion and the Search for Ultimate Reality* (Chicago: The University of Chicago, Phoenix Books, 1955), 11-12.

3. John Herman Randall, Jr., "The Ontology of Paul Tillich," in *The Theology of Paul Tillich,* ed. by Charles W. Kegley and Robert W. Bretall (New York: The Macmillan Company, 1964), 156.

4. Tillich, *Biblical Religion,* 14.

5. Tillich, *Systematic Theology,* I, 186-192.

6. *Ibid.,* I, 193. For Tillich's understanding of ultimate concern see in this same work, I, 11-14.

7. *Ibid.,* I, 186-189, 235-238.

8. *Ibid.,* I, 211.

9. *Ibid.,* III, 50-98.

10. Tillich, *Biblical Religion,* 11-12.

11. Ontology is the study of being.

12. Tillich, *Systematic Theology,* I, 71-83.

13. *Ibid.,* I, 98.

14. *Ibid.,* I, 94-100; 168-171.

15. Tillich, *Biblical Religion,* 5-20.

16. Tillich, *Systematic Theology,* I, 100-105.

17. *Ibid.,* I, 98-99.

18. *Ibid.,* I, 201-205.

19. See, for example, Charles Hartshorne's remarks in *Theology*

*of Paul Tillich, 188-190.*

20. *Ibid.*, I, 172-173, 272.

21. *Ibid.*, I, 205-210.

22. *Ibid.*, I, 109.

23. *Ibid.*, I, 108-116; III, 115, 337.

24. *Ibid.*, I, 114.

25. Tillich, *Theology of Culture,* 129. For Freud's view that only the religion of the common man should be called religion, see SE XXI, 74.

26. Tillich, *Systematic Theology,* I, 34-38, 129; III, 124-127.

27. *Ibid.*, I, 112-113; III, 118.

28. Homans, "Toward a Psychology of Religion," 63.

29. Tillich, *Systematic Theology,* III, 130-133.

30. Paul Tillich, *The Protestant Era* (Chicago: The University of Chicago Press, Phoenix Books, 1957), 80-81; *Systematic Theology,* III, 119, 143-144.

31. Tillich, *Systematic Theology,* I, 150-151; II, 91; III, 130; Paul Tillich, *On the Boundary* (New York: Charles Scribner's Sons, 1966), 64.

32. Tillich, *Systematic Theology,* I, 150-151; II, 91; III, 130; Paul Tillich, *On the Boundary* (New York: Charles Scribner's Sons, 1966), 64.

33. Paul Tillich, *Dynamics of Faith* (New York: Harper & Row Publishers, Inc., 1958), 41-48; *Systematic Theology,* I, 239-240.

34. Tillich, *Systematic Theology,* II, 9:

35. Paul Tillich, *Love, Power, and Justice* (London: Oxford University Press, 1954), 109.

36. Paul Tillich, "The Meaning and Justification of Religious Symbols," in *Religious Experience and Truth,* ed. by Sidney Hook (New York: New York University Press, 1961), 3-5; *Dynamics of Faith,* 41-42.

37. Tillich, *Courage to Be,* 182-190.

38. Tillich, *Theology of Culture,* 25; *Systematic Theology,* I, 245.

39. *Ibid.*, II, 80.

40. Tillich, *Dynamics of Faith,* 78.

41. Tillich, *Systematic Theology,* III, 100.

*CHAPTER FOUR*

# Tillich's Response to Freud's
# View of God and Religion

### I.

WHILE TILLICH ENDORSED OR SYMPATHIZED with a number of Freud's ideas, he found it necessary to chide Freud for surreptitiously introducing elements of faith into his purportedly scientific views about God, man, and religion. The proper competence of science is restricted by definition to empirical data. Consequently, whenever scientists give anwers to ultimate questions raised by empircal experience, they obtain their answers (including negative answers) from some philosophical or theological tradition which provides an interpretation of reality as a whole. These answers are based on presuppositions that are indemonstrable because they transcend the empirical realm.

Everyone chooses to "believe" in some such tradition and uses it, conciously or unconsciously, to supply answers to questions of higher value and meaning raised by empirical experience. A "faith" dimension, therefore, is involved in everyone's answers to ultimate questions. Even when scientists claim to be purely objective, they unconsciously bring to their analysis of empirical data a number of philosophical presuppositions drawn from the tradition of

40

interpreting reality which they personally have decided to embrace.[1]

Accordingly, whenever the personal faith of a scientist leads him to conclusions about *ultimate* reality that are contrary to the faith experience of a Christian, the Christian may reject the other faith position in favor of his own if he finds his own is more reasonable because better grounded in his experience:

> The naturalistic element which Freud carried from the nineteenth into the twentieth century, his basic puritanism with respect to love, his pessimism about culture, and his reduction of religion to ideological projection are all expressions of faith and not the result of scientific analysis. There is no reason to deny to a scholar who deals with man and his predicament the right to introduce elements of faith. But, if he attacks other forms of faith in the name of scientific psychology, as Freud and many of his followers do, he is confusing dimensions. In this case, those who represent another kind of faith are justified in resisting attacks. It is not always easy to distinguish the element of faith from the element of scientific hypothesis in a psychological assertion, but it is possible and often necessary.[2]

Exposing some of Freud's faulty presuppositions, however, does not invalidate everything he concluded about God and religion. Tillich agreed with Freud that the naive understanding of God, which thinks of him literally as a gigantic father figure residing somewhere in outer space, is patently infantile. Also mistaken is the notion that God intervenes regularly in human affairs to act in ways *contrary* to the laws of nature which God himself must uphold as creative ground.[3] It was admitted by Tillich that this understanding of God still prevails in some religious groups. He called this naive way of thinking *supranaturalism* (fundamentalism) and fought against it throughout his career:

> The main argument against it (supranaturalism) is that it transforms the infinity of God into a finiteness which is merely an extension of the categories of finitude. This is done in respect to space by establishing a supranatural divine world alongside the natural human world. . . . Against this kind of supranaturalism the arguments of naturalism are valid and, as such, represent the true concern of religion, the infinity of the infinite, and the inviolability of the created structures of the finite. Theology must accept the antisupranatural criticism of naturalism.[4]

Tillich also agreed with Freud that some of the images or symbols employed by religion are derived from childhood experiences retained unconsiously in memory. But Tillich understood such symbols in a positive way as indispensable tools for interpreting and relating to the mysterious dimension of the unconditional. As long as such figurative language is taken symbolically and not literally, it remains a valid (but historically conditioned) expression of man's experience of ultimate concern.[5]

## II.

A carefully reasoned answer was given by Tillich to Freud's claim that the idea of God is nothing more than the psychological projection of the father image deriving from childhood experience. He began by recalling that Freud:

> . . . calls God the projection of the father image. But every projection is not only a projection *of* something, it is also a projection *upon* something. What is this 'something' upon which the image of the father is 'projected' so that it becomes divine? The answer can only be: It is projected upon the 'screen' of the un-

conditional! And this screen is not projected. It makes projection possible. So we do not reject the theory of projection (which is as old as philosophical thought), but we try to refine it. . . . in three steps. The first and basic step is the assertion that man, as man, experiences something unconditional. . . . The second step is the recognition that the early dependence on the father, or on father figures, drives to a projection of the father image upon the screen of the unconditional. The third step is the insight that this indentification of the concrete media of the unconditional with the unconditioned itself is, religiously speaking, demonic, psychologically speaking, neurotic. Education and psychotherapy can and must dissolve this kind of father image, but they cannot dissolve the element of the unconditional itself. . . .[6]

Tillich agreed with Freud about the psychological mechanism of projection, but pointed out that there must always be something in reality to receive a projected image, otherwise it cannot be consciously experienced. This is also true of the projected father image in the idea of God. It is utilized symbolically to supply the concerete personal element without which a personal relationship with the unconditional would not be intelligible. The "something" which is present in reality like a *screen* able to receive the projected father image is man's subtle awareness of the ultimate ground of all that exists. This awareness needs to be clothed with something appropriately concrete to facilitate its accessibility to the finite mind of religiously concerned man:

. . . .projection is always projection *on* something—a wall, a screen, another being, another realm. Obviously, it is absurd to class that on which the projection is realized with the projection itself. A screen is not projected; it receives the projection. The realm

against which the divine images are projected is not itself a projection. It is the experienced ultimacy of
being and meaning. It is the realm of ultimate concern.[7]

It was suggested by Tillich (with obvious indebtedness
to Freud) that there is something in the very nature of the
way man begins to experience social reality that makes the
archetypal father image (after the matriarchal stage of historical consciousness) an inevitable and necessarily
religious paradigm for understanding his personal
relationship with the transpersonal reality of the divine
ground.[8]

Since the creative ground of everthing personal cannot
be thought of as less than personal, man has learned historically to prefer personal symbols to interpret his relationship
with the unconditional. The personal symbol chosen by the
Judeo-Christian tradition as most appropriate for mediating
an understanding of this unique relationship is the father
image derived primarily from early childhood. This image
was intuitively elected because, in post-matriarchal
societies, it is ordinarily the most powerful personal image
present in human experience; the father of one's infancy is
remembered unconsiously in the light of archetypal magic
as omnipotent (protector even of the powerful mother), omniscient, lovingly provident, and requiring reponsibility of
his offspring. The powerful mother of early childhood experience shares all of these attributes with the father, but it
is the common experience of children that even she is afraid
to go some places, especially at night, unless accompanied
by the father.

Nevertheless, Tillich warned, it would be wrong to identify the concrete element in the idea of God with its ultimate
referent, the unconditional. To do so would demonically distort a fundamental religious symbol and involve the
prepetuation of an infantile attitude fostering neurotic

dependence, as Freud correctly observed.

Tillich also concurred with Freud's view that the super-ego, constituted by introjected parental attitudes, is the unconscious source of the traditional religious commandments which express man's recognition of the need for moral standards. For Tillich, however, the moral imperative (human awareness of the unconditional demand that the rights of other persons should be respected) always includes an implicit awareness of the unconditional mystery who is morality's ultimate sanction.[9] The moral imperative itself is an unchanging absolute in human experience. But the *specific contents* of the moral imperative which are given expression in traditional moral standards represent historically limited interpretations which, in time, must be transcended under the impetus of increased understanding. The dialectical development of moral insight called forth by the human capacity for self-transcendence and the lure of the unconditional results in what Tillich approvingly called *transmoral* morality (morality intent on surpassing its past inadequacies).[10]

## III.

Freud argued that mythological religious interpretations of reality had to be abandoned completely if man was to progress to intellectural maturity.[11] He conceded that religious conceptions had once served a civilizing purpose when no better means of fostering morality and stability within society had been available. He also acknowledged that it would be disastrous to remove the civilizing influence of religion before replacing it with a scientific viewpoint better able to motivate the masses to maintain moral standards. To achieve that goal, Freud believed that those who are scientifically educated should strive to emancipate the masses from infantile religious beliefs.[12]

Tillich agreed with Freud that ingenuous understandings

of God and religion should be replaced by a mature view of reality. But for Tillich this mature view of reality should include a mature understanding of God as the answer to man's ultimate questions. In attempting to interpret his experience of unconditional mystery, primitive man did invent mythological stories which gave symbolic expression to his historically conditioned insights. Nevertheless, primitive man could not invent the unconditional mystery which he was pointing to with his myths, for the unconditional is experienced as the ultimate ground of the human mind that attempts to explain it.[13]

Two stages of literalism were distinguished by Tillich in man's historical understanding of myth. In the first, or natural stage, which is characteristic of man at the precritical level, the mythical and literal are not distinguished because the possibilty (or need) of doing so is not yet recognized. The second, or reactive stage, is characteristic of postcritical man, who has begun to experience the religious answers formulated by past ages as problematic but defensively supresses his doubts instead of honestly facing them and searching for a nonliteral (symbolic) way to understand the genuine religious meaning of myth.[14]

## IV.

Well-intentioned religious leaders sometimes mistakenly assume that if mythical language is deliteralized it becomes meaningless and must be abandoned. Since they intuitively realize that the concrete language of myth (poetic symbolism) is the only way religion can speak meaningfully about its experience of the unconditional, they defensively reject all scientific criticism of literally intended mythical language, even when this criticism is justified. As a consequence, the reactionary religious statements made by such people sound more and more divorced from the world of real experience.

Tillich agreed that religion must use the concrete language of myth to express experience of ulitmate concern, but pointed out that religious myth can, and eventually must, be broken (deliteralized) even though it cannot be dispensed with:

> The mythical consciousness can therefore be either broken or unbroken; in any case, it does not disappear. If one decides to characterize only the unbroken mythical mentality as mythical, then of course the myth is overcome in religion and it is shown to be nonessential. If, on the other hand, one calls every intuition of transcendence mythical, then there is no such thing as an unmythical attitude and the myth is shown to be essential.[15]

It followed for Tillich that theology, in a postcritical age, has an obligation to be critical of outmoded religious understandings, and to insist on deliteralizing the mythical religious viewpoint of earlier ages. Traditional attempts to defend a literal understanding of religious symbols have been challenged and discredited by the scientific and demythologizing spirit of the modern age. This criticism also has rendered problematic earlier theological statements formulated when a literal reading of religious symbols in the Bible was still natural and unquestioned. It is not only traditonal religious symbols that need to deliteralized; traditional *doctrines* based on a literal understanding of such symbols must also be hermenueutically qualified.

While Tillich acknowledged the validity of the demand for demythologizing, he also recognized that such an antithetical demand can sometimes become the opposite form of the error it reacts against. In that event the genuine gain in insight which originally motivated the demand for change can be lost, along with whatever degree of truth was present in the older viewpoint it strives to replace.[16]

Consequently, Tillich said *yes* to the relative kind of

demythologizing that preserves the valid substance of traditional beliefs, but *no* to the absolute kind of demythologizing which can be as intolerant and blind as some outmoded religious veiws.

## V.

Whether one decides to agree with Freud that the idea of God is merely a projection of the father image, or with Tillich, that the father image is the archetypal symbol especially appropriate for pointing to man's experience of the unconditional, will depend upon whether or not one has become consciously aware of one's relationship with unconditional mystery in the experience called faith. At this point one can hear the voice of Freud reply:

> If the truth of religious doctrines is dependent on an inner experience which bears witness to that truth, what is one to do about the many people who do not have this rare experience? One may require every man to use the gift of reason which he possesses, but one cannot erect, on the basis of a motive that exists only for a very few, an obligation that shall apply to everyone. If one man has gained an unshakable conviction of the true reality of religious doctrines from a state of ecstasy which has deeply moved him, of what significance is that to others?[17]

In response to such questions, Tillich replied that no religious group has the right to impose its special beliefs on persons who do not freely accept them. Whenever a religious group presumes to have such a right, it acts demonically by mistakenly elevating to the level of the absolute its merely relative power to establish reasonable norms for its own freely consenting members. As a member of a minority group discriminated against for centuries by distorted understandings of Christianity, Freud could only applaud Tillich's position.

Tillich would also insist that the term "reason" in Freud's statement above should be understood as including the broader philosophical insights of "ontological" reason as well as the narrower scientific observations of "technical" reason.[18]

More to the point, Tillich would lament that Freud's understanding of religious faith suffered from several popular misconceptions, and this is hardly suprising, for:

> Today the term "faith" is more productive of disease than of health. It confuses, misleads, creates alternately skepticism and fanaticism, intellectual resistance and emotional surrender, rejection of genuine religion and subjection to substitutes. Indeed, one is tempted to suggest that the word "faith" should be dropped completely; but desirable as that may be it is hardly possible. A powerful tradition protects it. And there is as yet no substitute expressing the reality to which "faith" points. So for the time being, the only way of dealing with the problem is to try to reinterpret the word and remove the confusing and distorting connotations, some of which are the heritage of centuries.[19]

If faith is correctly understood, it is, according to Tillich, neither "a rare experience" nor "a state of ecstasy." It is true that genuine faith experience does contain an "ecstatic" element; that is, it does, be it ever so briefly and fragmentarily, enable human reason to transcend (or stand outside of) its ordinary mode of knowing within the subject-object structure of reality and thereby become aware of the dimension of the unconditional. But such an experience should not be thought of as involving an acute emotional upheaval that leads to dramatic conversion.[20] Such a conversion sometimes does accompany the experience of faith, but, ordinarily, this is not the case. Faith experience can come about gradually or suddenly in life and can range all the way from a fleeting (but profound) awareness, lasting only a few seconds, to the fullblown ecstasy of the classical mystics, which is certainly extraordinary in measure and not to be taken as the criterion for ordinary faith experience.[21]

The experience called religious faith occurs when man is grasped in his personal center by an awareness of the unconditional mystery which grounds and transcends the universe. Once man encounters this unconditional creative ground it becomes a matter of ultimate concern for him, for he realizes that it is the source of his own being and the ultimate aim of his capacity for self-transcendence.[22]

If a man has been raised within a monotheistic religious tradition and was exposed in a positive way to the language it employs to interpret the unconditional, he will predictably use the word "God" to name the transcendent power and meaning which he has experienced. But this is not necessarily the case. If his exposure to traditional religious symbols was nil or unduly negative, he will find it necessary to name the unconditional with terms drawn from some other tradition of interpreting reality which he has found meaningful (art, philosophy, natural science).

For this reason it was suggested by Tillich that Albert Einstein, who once denied the idea of a personal God in a paper he publicly delivered, seems, upon closer examination, to have been really denying a literal belief in the mythological understanding of God which still prevades the popular religious imagination. If other statements which Einstein made on the same occasion are examined closely, they seem to indicate awareness of a transcendent dimension of creative power and reason present in the universe, filling it with mysterious order and purpose.

It would seem, then, that Einstein was grasped with ultimate concern for something unconditional which he thought of in terms of transcendent reason and order – the very things to which Einstein seems to have committed his life. If this was so, Tillich concluded, such commitment was religious in the broad sense and Einstein implicitly acknowledged and served God (the God beyond God who is really God) but as known by another name, taken from a more meaningful tradition.[23]

## VI.

This same line of reasoning explicitly used by Tillich in the case of Einstein can be used implicitly with reference to Freud, who also publicly rejected the idea of a personal God. If the thought of Freud is considered carefully, it becomes apparent that he, too, emphatically rejected the mythological God. Furthermore, Freud speculated about the ultimate meaning of civilization in the following way:

> . . . I was led to the idea that civilization is a process in the service of Eros, whose purpose it is to combine single human individuals, and after that families, then races, peoples and nations, into one great unity, the unity of mankind. Why this has to happen we do not know; the work of Eros is precisely this.[24]

Judging from these words, it would seem that Freud was aware of a mysterious dimension of power which manifests its purposive presence within finite reality and yet trancends it. In another place Freud referred to "eternal Eros," the "preserver of all things."[25] Although admittedly involving ambiguity, such statements seem to suggest that Freud, too, had been grasped by the awareness of something he regarded with ultimate seriousness, because it seemed to be the mysterious source of eventual fulfillment for mankind. Freud also seems to have committed himself to the service of this transcendent Eros and to have striven to free mankind from the pathological aggressiveness which he considered the chief obstacle to its becoming "one great unity."[26]

In addition to the lofty thoughts about Eros quoted

above, Freud made the following remarks in praise of Logos, or reason:

> The voice of intellect is a soft one, but it does not rest till it has gained a hearing. Finally, after a countless succession of rebuffs, it succeeds. This is one of the few points on which one may be optimistic about the future of mankind, but it is in itself a point of no small importance. And from it one can derive yet other hopes. The primacy of the intellect lies, it is true, in a distant, distant future, but probably not in an *infinitely* distant one. It will presumably set itself the same aims as those whose realization you expect from your God. . . . Our god, Logos, will fulfill whichever of these wishes nature outside us allows, but he will do it very gradually, only in the unforeseeable future, and for a new generation of men.[27]

In this remarkable passage (redolent of prophetic eschatology) Freud recited the credo of his own faith, scientism.

Logos and Eros, then, seem to have been names for that which concerned Freud ultimately. But that should come as no surprise, Tillich would remark, because Reason, Truth, and Love have been other names for God throughout much of religious history.[28]

Tillich would have been sympathetic to the view that Freud's atheism was an epiphenomenon precipitated by the distortions present in his negative exposure to traditional religious symbols. Stated otherwise, it is possible to view Freud's unbelief as akin to that paradoxical atheism which accompanies religion throughout history and says *no* to its demonic distortions of religious symbols.[29] Freud spoke an emphatic *no* against literal belief in the mythological God and its regressive consequences. Such protest was endorsed by Tillich, who went on to observe:

It is regrettable that scientists believe that they have refuted religion when they rightly have shown that there is no evidence whatsoever for the assumption that such a being (the mythological God) exists. Actually, they have not only not refuted religion, but they have done it a considerable service. They have forced it to reconsider and to restate the meaining of the tremendous word *God*.[30]

While it seems likely that Tillich would have numbered Freud among those humaninsts whose "secular faith"[31] indicates that they are religious in the broad sense of the term, he also would have agreed that Freud's own humanistic religion, scientism, was demonically distorted. In his well-intentioned attempt to combat what he understood to be error, Freud antithetically claimed too much for scientific method and fell into error himself by elevating something relative and conditional to the level of the unconditional.[32]

## VII.

Although Tillich agreed with Freud in part about the role that fantasy and projection play in the creation of symbols and myths, he did not agree with Freud's conclusion that all religious beliefs are merely *illusions* based on infantile wishes. He granted that a naive interpretation of traditional religious symbols can result in the mistaken expectation that unfounded hopes and desires will be actualized. An example would be the unschooled assumption that the symbols of eschatological hope in the Bible will be fulfilled literally (instead of symbolically and essentially) at the end of time.[33]

To help clarify this problem, Tillich made a distinction between hope for future fulfillment which has some basis in reality and that which does not. Freud insisted that something wished for must have an *experimental* basis in reality before one can realistically hope for its fulfillment. Tillich disagreed; he reasoned that verification can be *experiential* as well as experimental.[34] Therefore, to hope for the future fulfillment of a wish experienced as having a genuine (albeit transempirical) basis in reality would not be the same as pursuing an illusion.

On the strength of Freud's own views Tillich would reproach him as having been deceptively vague and somewhat inconsistent when he said, "What is characteristic of illusions is that they are derived from human wishes."[35] Tillich would counterpose that it is also characteristic of creative discoveries of the new that they are derived from human wishes. To buttress this position he would appeal to Freud's observation that civilization achieves progress on the basis of neurotic discontent. It is the person who is not psychologically well adjusted to a difficult state of reality who is more likely to sublimate by striving to discover and actuate new possibilities that would improve his lot.[36] While basically agreeing with this notion of Freud's,[37] Tillich qualified it by noting that neurosis is not the cause of sublimation but the occasion. The cause is human freedom (denied by Freud) and its relative power to transcend the source of neurotic conflict in search of some new and acceptable way of investing frustrated psychic energy.[38]

The progress that results from all creative striving clearly involves the fulfillment of wishes projected into the future as possibilities intuitively recognized as achievable. Therefore, some of what Freud called illusions are conscious longings for the actualization of real possibilities implicit in human experience.[39]

For example, Tillich would reject as misleading Freud's statement that "it was an illusion of Columbus's that he had discovered a new sea-route to the Indies. The part played by his wish in this error is very clear."[40] It is true that when Columbus discovered the New World he concluded mistakenly that he had arrived at the East Indies. But his fundamental intuition that a new sea route to the Indies was discoverable was not an unfounded illusion. Later explorations proved that it was correct. On the basis of his experience of maritime and geographical reality, Columbus realized that his wish to find a new sea route to the Indies was a *real* possibility. Because his intuition was basically correct, his wish that such a sea route might be discovered was eventually fulfilled by Magellan. In the final analysis, what Columbus had believed in and hoped for was not an illusion.

The same is analogously true, Tillich would say, of man's religious experience of encounter with God and its implicit promise of fulfillment beyond death. One who has been grasped by personal awareness of the unconditional manifesting itself to him as the ground and *aim* of his being has a real basis in his experience[41] for concluding that God's self-gift to man is an *invitational* communcation of transcendent (death-transcending) love.

When man is borne experientially (even though fleetingly and fragmentarily) into transcendent union with unconditional love, this says something profoundly meaningful and reassuring to the intuition of the one so grasped. Such experience implies that the transcendent other who takes the initiative by giving himself to man *temporally* in the encounter of faith is thereby indicating that he intends to give himself to man *eternally* (beyond the transitional event of death) in a union that will fulfill man's deepest yearning for lasting participation in unconditional meaning and love.

The only way that man can give concrete expression to his divinely encouraged anticipation of ultimate fulfillment is by having recourse to his creative imagination. There the archetypal paradigms of union and fulfillment are available for refashioning as religious symbols which analogically enable man to understand something of his sublime relationship with the unconditional. It is man's appointed lot to keep refashioning these powerful mythical images into increasingly adequate bearers of religious meaning.[43] The sacred marriage between father sky and mother earth celebrated by archaic societies was destined to give way to the Christian view that all who are open to transcendent truth and love are called by the bridegroom Word of God (Jn. 3:29) to participate in the great marriage between heaven and earth (Rev. 19:6-9; 21:1-4).

Correspondingly, there is a way in which the symbol system created by Freud to explain his experience of transempirical psychic reality also can be called a mythology. He himself said so and warned that the symbols used as hypothetical constructs in his psychoanalytic myths should not be reified.[44] Yet, on the basis of his personal experience, Freud never doubted that these symbolic constructs point to something real, albeit transempirical. The Freudian myth has convincing power precisely because we are aware that we indirectly experience a realm of psychic reality that corresponds essentially to the Freudian symbols. So, likewise, religious symbols have compelling power for religiously engaged man because he has personally experienced the transcendent reality to which these symbols point, and he, also, cannot doubt their ultimate referent.

## NOTES

1. Tillich, *Dynamics of Faith,* 92-93; Raphael Demos, "Religious Faith and Scientific Faith," in *Religious Experience and Truth,* ed. by Sidney Hook (New York: New York University Press, 1961), 130-136. Freud acknowledged that there is an element of faith present in scientific hypothesizing. See SE XVIII, 59-60.

2. Tillich *Dynamics of Faith,* 84, 126-127.

3. Tillich *Systematic Theology,* I, 115-117.

4. *Ibid.,* II, 6.

5. *Ibid.,* I, 239-241.

6. Tillich, *Theology of Culture,* 140. Although Freud would

agree that in most cases projection involves an extramental referent, he also described a kind of projection (involved in the anxiety neuroses) in which a feeling of impending doom or expectant dread is projected onto external reality in general in a way that dispenses with any specific concrete referent (SE XVI, 398, 401-402; XXII, 82-83). But this atypical kind of projection which dispenses with perceptual elements is clearly not the kind that Freud had in mind when he talked about the religious experience of God. When discussing this matter Freud repeatedly stated that man personifies "the forces of nature." See SE XXI, 15-24, esp. 22.

7. Tillich, *Systematic Theology*, I, 212. It is possible that Tillich was indebted to Heidegger for this insight. In *Being and Time* (New York: Harper & Row Publishers, Inc., 1962, 370-371), Heidegger makes the following observation:

> ... meaning is that wherein the understandability of somthing maintains itself – even that of something which does not come into view explicitly and thematically. 'Meaning' signifies the 'upon-which' [Woraufhin] of a primary projection in terms of which something can be concieved in its possibility as that which it is. Projection discloses possibilities – that is to say, it discloses the sort of thing that makes possible.
>
> to lay bare the 'upon-which' of a projection, amounts to disclosing that which makes possible what has been projected.

In the course of explaining Freud's theories Ernest Jones also spoke of a "screen" upon which fantasies are projected. See his *Life and Work of Sigmund Freud*, I, 322.

8. Tillich, "The Religious Symbol," 305.

9. Tillich, *Systematic Theolgy*, III, 38-50.

10. Paul Tillich, *My Search for Absolutes* (New York: Simon & Schuster, Inc., Credo Perspectives, 1969), 92-112; "The Transmoral Conscience," in *Morality and Beyond* (Harper & Row Publishers, Inc., 1966), 65-81, esp. 77, 80-81; Systematic Theology, I, 125; III, 159-160, 232, 266, 271-275, 294, 333; *Love, Power, and Justice*, 76-77, 80-82; *Dynamics of Faith*, 5-6; *Theology of Culture*, 133-141.

11. SE XXII, 160-175.

12. *Ibid.*, XXI, 38-39, 48-49, 74-77.

13. Tillich, *Theology of Culture*, 128.

14. Tillich, *Dynamics of Faith*, 52-53.

15. Tillich, "The Religious Symbol," 310.

16. Tillich, *Systematic Theology*, III, 343-344.

17. SE XXI, 28.

18. Ontological and Technical reason were explained in the preceding chapter, 24-29.

19. Tillich, *Dynamics of Faith,* ix; see also *Systematic Theology,* III, 130.

20. Tillich, *Dynamics of Faith,* 6-7.

21. Paul Tillich, *Ultimate Concern: Tillich in Dialogue,* ed. by D. Mackenzie Brown (New York: Harper & Row Publishers, Inc., Harper Colophon Books, 1965), 8-9; *Systematic Theology,* II, 242.

22. Tillich, *Theology of Culture,* 22-29; *Dynamics of Faith,* 8-16.

23. Tillich, *Theology of Culture,* 127-132.

24. SE, XXI, 122.

25. Ibid., XXI, 145; XI, 70.

26. Tillich, *Systematic Theology,* III, 356-361. Oskar Pfister expressed much the same view in one of his letters to Freud. See *Psychoanalysis and Faith, the Letters of Sigmund Freud and Oskar Pfister,* ed, by Heinrich Meng and Ernst L. Freud (New York: Basic Books, Inc., 1964), 63.

27. SE XXI, 53-54.

28. Tillich, *Dynamics of Faith,* 47.

29. Tillich, *Theology of Culture,* 25.

30. *Ibid.,* 5.

31. Tillich, *Dynamics of Faith,* 63.

32. Tillich, *Systematic Theology,* III, 103.

33. *Ibid.,* III, 397, 423; *Dynamics of Faith,* 104.

34. This important distinction was explained in Chapter III, 29-30.

35. SE XXI, 30-31.

36. *Ibid.,* XI, 131-137; XXI, 90-91.

37. Tillich, *Systematic Theology,* III, 308.

38. Tillich, "Existentialism and Psychotherapy," 11-12; *Courage to Be,* 67-69; *Systematic Theology,* III, 308, 329. Freud acknowleged that there is something about artistic creativity which his psychonalytic theory could not account for. See SE XI, 135-136.

39. Tillich, *Systematic Theology,* III, 303-304, 317-320. Herbert Marcuse has also faulted Freud's failure to recognize adequately the basically creative function of human wishing. See his *Eros and*

*Civilization* (New York: Random House, Inc., Vintage Books, 1955), 130, 132-133,169.

40. SE XXI, 30.

41. Tillich, *Systematic Theology*, I, 109-110. Tillich would say, more technically, that when such revelatory experience occurs (and all faith experience is in some degree revelatory) ontological reason in man is swept ecstatically into union with being-itself – or the divine ground – and is then functioning with its essential perfection in a way that (briefly and fragmentarily) overcomes the enstrangement and ambiquity that ordinarily distort its functioning under the conditions of existence. See his *Systematic Theology*, III, 129-131, 134-135.

42. *Ibid.*, III, 129-138.

43. See Erich Neumann's *The Origins and History of Consciousness* (Princeton, New Jersey: Princeton University Press, 1954), passim.

44. Tillich, "The Religious Symbol," 310-314. Freud himself referred to his theory of the instincts as a mythology. See SE XXII, 95.

*CHAPTER FIVE*

# Summary and Conclusion

WE HAVE SEEN IN THE PRECEDING THREE chapters that Tillich accepted various of Freud's observations about traditional religious beliefs. Because of the number and complexity of these observations, it seems appropriate to summarize them for the reader:

1. There *is* an important connection between the Oedipus complex and the historical development of religion and morality.

2. The nature of early childhood experience is such (in post-matriarchal societies) that God *is* inevitably thought of as "Father" later in life.

3. The psycholgical projection of the father image *is* involved in the idea of God.

4. Belief in God which thinks of him literally as a mythologically conceived father figure *is* infantile and neurotic.

5. There *is* no evidence for the existence of the literally

conceived mythological God.

6. The existence (or reality) of God *cannot* be proved (demonstrated).

7. Subjecting oneself uncritically to the mythologically conceived authority of the Father-God *does* result in an infantile dependence which impedes maturity and the full acceptance of adult responsibility.

8. Attempts made to prove the authority of the Bible by appealing to statements and events found within the Bible *are* unconvincing.

9. Personal religious experience *is not* something that can be appealed to in order to prove to another the truth of religious beliefs.

10. A literal belief in the mythological statements found in the Bible *is* naively mistaken.

11. The claim that religious beliefs contrary to reason should be believed *is* absurd.

While Tillich agreed with Freud on all the above-listed positions, he disagreed about the following:

1. *Freud's position:* Scientific methodology (experimental verification) is the only permissible means of determining truth.

   *Tillich's response:* the *experimental* verification of scientific methodology is not the only means of determining truth. The *experiential* verification employed by ontological reason and religious faith is also a valid means of arriving at knowledge of the truth (even though indirectly known truth, which transcends the empirical, retains an element of mystery and ambiguity because its adequate expression is something we are always only approximating).

2. *Freud's position:* Philosophical intuition cannot guide man to genuine truth.

   *Tillich's response:* Philosophical intuition can guide man to an approximate kind of knowledge about indirectly experienceable realities. Such inferred knowledge does involve an element of obscurity and is always subject to further clarification in the light of increased understanding, but man knows the transempirical realities being clarified are truly present in his experience.

3. *Freud's position:* Metaphysics has evolved from and is still essentially related to mythology. Both provide illusory interpretations of reality based on expectations which are nothing more than infantile wish fulfillment. The interpretations of reality provided by metaphysics are more abstract than those of mythology, but based on illusions and infantile wishes, nevertheless. Both metaphysics and mythology can ultimately be reduced to psychic elements present in the human unconscious, i.e., to metapsychology.

   *Tillich's response:* Metaphysical constructs have evolved historically from mythological constructs, and sometimes do involve cognitive elements in the service of wish fulfillment. But interpretations of reality arrived at under the impetus of wish fulfillment are not necessarily illusory, since creative desire for the actuation of new possibilities underlies all human progress. What ultimately matters is whether or not human wishes have some basis in experienceable reality. Such a basis can be *experientially* verified even if it is not experimentally verifiable.

   Metaphysical and mythological constructs are not able to be accounted for merely by positing the influence of unconscious psychological factors. Such constructs are basically engendered by man's attempts to understand his experience of the unconditional power and meaning upon which even finite psychological powers ultimately depend.

4. *Freud's position:* There is no valid knowledge which derives from revelation.

   *Tillich's response:* The experience of revelation does result in genuine knowledge about the self-manifestation of the divine ground to man, but nothing is empirically observed or divinely dictated when unconditional mystery discloses itself. What is written in sacred scripture was humanly realized about the divine mystery when this mystery manifested itself to human consciousness with revelatory impact.

5. *Freud's position:* The Bible contains no real truth about ultimate reality. It is merely an ancient expression of wish fulfilment.

   *Tillich's response:* Sacred scripture does not contain divinely dictated truths, but it does contain divinely inspired insights into the divine-human relationship arrived at under the impact of the self-manifestations of the unconditional.

6. Freud's position: Personal religious experience is nothing but subjective feeling; the religious beliefs stemming from it can be explained entirely in terms of psychological processes.

   *Tillich's response:* It is doubtlessly true that sometimes what people think of as religious experience is merely subjective feeling. Genuine religious experience however, involves the total person on all levels of his being and always includes (however obscurely or fleetingly) an awareness of something unconditional that transcends finite psychological processes (and is their ultimate ground).

7. *Freud's position:* All religious beliefs are illusions.

   *Tillich's response:* Only superstitious religious beliefs which are contrary to reason, or have no real basis in human experience, are illusions.

8. *Freud's position:* All forms of religion are infantile.

   *Tillich's response:* Only distorted forms of religion which cling regressively to outdated notions and persist in identifying the conditional with the unconditional are infantile. Forms of religious belief which abjure regressive distortion and encourage self-transcendence are creative interpretations of man's experience of the unconditional.

9. *Freud's position:* Modern man should eliminate religious myth entirely from his understanding of reality, because it contains superstitious and unfounded beliefs invented by primitive man.

   *Tillich's response:* Modern man's religious beliefs should be demythologized (deliteralized) and made compatible with contemporary advances in understanding, but such demythologizing should be relative in scope and intent, not absolute. The valid insights which underlie mythical symbols should be preserved and the viable symbols retained, for religion will always have a reasonable need to interpret its experience of unconditional mystery with concrete symbols. Primitive man did invent the myths (symbolic stories) which expressed his ultimate concern, but he could not invent his awareness of the unconditional ground of being and meaning which he was pointing to with his myths.

10. *Freud's position:* The idea of God is merely a psychological projection of the father image of early childhood; it has no real ultimate referent.

    *Tillich's response:* the idea of God necessarily involves a symbolic and nonsymbolic element. The symbolic element ordinarily used in the Judeo-Christian tradition is the father image, but it is merely a concrete medium of understanding which points beyond itself to the experience of unconditional being and meaning ultimately intended by the word "God." When the concrete father image is used to point to the mystery of God, it *is* projected psychologically. But since there must always be something present in reality to receive a projected image (like a screen) in order for it to be experienced as real, it is the "screen" of the unconditional which receives the projected father image used by man to point to his experienced relationship with the transpersonal ground of his personal being.

11. *Freud's position:* The Ten Commandments which religion claims to have received from God are in reality the precipitate of parental commands retained in the superego and reinforced by traditional social sanctions. Primitive man created a mythological explanation of the origin of these commandments to enhance their authority and insure their observance. He thereby hoped to maintain established order within his society and to ward of the evils which he superstitiously thought of as divine punishment for wrongdoing.

    *Tillich's response:* It is true that the commandments of God were derived historically from the parental education of the superego within human society. It is also true that earlier and less developed stages of human understanding mistakenly interpreted natural events as punitive acts of God. That, however, in no way invalidates the fundamentally correct realization of past ages that the ultimate source of man's reason and freedom of choice certainly intends man to use this power in a way that will creatively enhance rather than destroy or diminish the sense of right order necessary for maintaining human community. And that inspired insight is what the Ten Commandments essentially express.

Since God is ultimately the source of the power that enables man to creatively recognize and teach others about moral responsibility, it is understandable and correct for primitive man to have created a myth (primitive explanation) which teaches that the Creator is the ultimate sanction for moral responsibility and wishes man to respond responsibly by treating other persons as he himself would like to be treated.

12. *Freud's position:* Belief in some form of final justice and unending life beyond death is merely an expression of infantile wish fulfillment: ". . . it would be very nice if there were a God who created the world and was a benevolent Providence, and if there were a moral order in the universe and an afterlife; but it is a very striking fact that all this is exactly as we are bound to wish it to be"[1]

*Tillich's response:* It is quite true that man *is bound* to wish for ultimate meaning and fulfillment beyond death; everything about him indicates that this is his destiny. The fact that man can think about the possibility of participating in the infinity and eternity of his creative ground indicates that he already has the capacity to do so. Man would not have been given the power to transcend himself unlimitedly in the direction of the unconditional mystery which grounds him and his universe if eternal life in communion with his unconditional ground were not his destiny. Eternal life, however, will not be a mere continuation beyond death of the life we now experience (as popular imagination frequently assumes). Eternal life will transcend temporal life and its physical limitations.[2]

In addition, man's experience of the unconditional demand present in the moral imperative implies that there is an ultimate justice which in some mysterious way finally rights all of the wrongs with which his present existence abounds; otherwise, his experience of freedom, justice, and responsibility would be meaningless and absurd.

It is his faith experience of a loving personal relationship with the creative ground of his capacity for ultimate meaning and fulfillment that assures man within time that he is destined to participate in these things eternally in communion with his creative ground.

13. *Freud's position:* Organized religion is a form of social manipulation fostered by the arbiters of civilization (those who wield political and economic power) so that the masses can be coerced more readily into submission; in return for enduring the frustration of their instinctual desires and political will, religion promises them an eternal reward after death.

*Tillich's response:* Religion has been and, doubtlessly, still is used by some as a means of influencing the masses to endure social injustice and political oppression. Such an occurrence is an example of the tragic ambiguity that plagues religion under the conditions of existence. But in its finer moments, religion has been the prime source of prophetic protest against injustice and oppression throughout history.

When religion fails in its duty to protest against social injustice, a conscious or unconscious awareness of transcendent justice can motivate a secular prophet like Karl Marx to say and do on behalf of the oppressed what religion has failed to say and do.[3] Nevertheless, Marx the secular prophet was a spiritual descendent of Amos the religious prophet, and availed himself of the traditional language of social protest that originated with religion.[4]

*In conclusion,* the reader should now be in a position to appreciate that Tillich has rendered a truly significant service to the Christian theological tradition by engaging in dialogue with the Freudian critique of religion. He has provided theology with perceptive distinctions between the negative part of Freud's thought that errs by excess, and the positive part that remains illuminatingly compatible with Christian faith experience.

The thing that is probably most striking to the person initially encountering this dialogue is the unexpected measure of Tillich's agreement with Freud – not the fact that he said an expected *no* to Freud, but the extent to which he also said *yes.* Tillich acknowledged a debt of gratitude to Freud for providing Christian theology with a number of valuable insights, but especially for enabling it to better recognize the unconscious psychological factors that can motivate religious man to seek a false and idolatrous security in his relationship with God. After Freud, such infantile dishonesty becomes more difficult to sustain, and theology is better able to understand not only man's need to *deliteralize* his religious symbols, but also the neurotic *resistance* such efforts regularly incur.

## NOTES

1. SE XXI, 33; See also XXIII, 211-212.

2. Tillich, *Systematic Theology,* I, 190-191, 206; III, 403-423.

3. Paul Tillich, *On the Boundry: An Autobiographical Sketch,* (New York: Scirbner's, 1966), 84-90; *The Socialist Decision,* (New York: Harper & Row, 1977), 100-112.

4. Paul Tillich, "Marx and the Prophetic Tradition," *Radical Religion,* (Autumn, 1935), I, 21-29.

# INDEX

V